DAYS THAT CHANGED THE WORLD

THE DAY THE WORLD STOOD STILL
SEPTEMBER 11th

Fiona Macdonald

ticktock
MEDIA

Copyright © ticktock Entertainment Ltd 2003
First published in Great Britain in 2003 by ticktock Media Ltd.,
Unit 2, Orchard Business Centre, North Farm Road, Tunbridge Wells, Kent, TN2 3XF
ISBN 1 86007 419 7 pbk
ISBN 1 86007 426 X hbk
Printed in Taiwan
A CIP catalogue record for this book is available from the British Library.

CONTENTS

INTRODUCTION *4–7*

BEFORE *culture clash* *8–15*

FEELINGS OF CHANGE *violent struggle* *16–21*

THE CRITICAL MOMENT *september 11th* *22–29*

AFTERMATH *climate of fear* *30–33*

LATER *the war on terror* *34–39*

FUTURE *the way ahead* *40–41*

TIMELINE *42–43*

GLOSSARY *44–45*

INDEX *46–47*

ACKNOWLEDGEMENTS *48*

The South Tower of the World Trade Center is engulfed in flame as the second plane hits its target.

Tuesday September 11th, 2001 has been called 'America's Day of Terror'. It was the day when more than 5,000 people – mostly American citizens – were horrifically killed or injured while peacefully going about their everyday business. It was the world's worst single terrorist act, and the first major terrorist attack on American soil.

Americans have always flown their flag proudly, but September 11th made many consider how others viewed their country for perhaps the first time.

Some of the victims were passengers in aircraft, hijacked by terrorists before they were deliberately flown into their respective targets. Others were police, ambulance crews and firefighters, who had hurried to the scene to help save lives and were caught up in the disaster when the World Trade Center towers collapsed to the ground. But most were regular office staff, ranging from senior executives to junior clerks and cleaners. They worked at the Pentagon, the U.S. Defense Department's headquarters just outside Washington DC, and for many well-known companies who rented office suites in the World Trade Center – two tall, slim towers that rose high above the business district and dominated the skyline of New York, America's most important commercial city.

The deaths of so many innocent people shocked the whole world. Millions watched in horror and disbelief as the tragedy in New York unfolded before their very eyes, live on television. Thousands of other people logged on to the Internet as well, in order to keep abreast of the

After the attack, America turned all of its sophisticated weaponry, such as this B-2 Stealth Bomber, to finding and attacking those it believed were responsible for the atrocity.

events as they happened.

All of these people were powerless to help but too stunned to switch off their screens. At first, people could not believe what they were seeing, but then the awful truth became clear. This was not a disaster movie, with special effects created on a computer. It was real life, and it was terrible. But who had caused it and why?

The events of September 11th created a new sense of fear, bewilderment and uncertainty in America – a country not

used to living with the fear of potential terrorist attacks. This was coupled with further attacks in the form of sinister packages containing spores of the deadly germ anthrax, which added to the feelings of anxiety. But this was not only an American tragedy – people of many nationalities were killed in the attacks. It affected many other countries too, and changed the pattern of international relationships for ever. It profoundly altered American people's view of themselves,

An exhausted New York firefighter reflects on the events of the day, September 11th, 2001.

INTRODUCTION

Kofi Annan is the leader of the United Nations. The organisation found itself caught in the middle during the 2003 Iraq war.

After America had toppled the Taliban in Afghanistan, they turned their attention to Iraq, led by Saddam Hussein. Some Americans thought he may have played a part in the September 11th attacks.

their country and the world, and it led to a new, tougher role for America in world politics as they hunted for those people they believed were responsible for the atrocity.

Attention focused on the Middle East, a region lying between Africa and Asia. Here, many people were upset by America's involvement in the region and its apparent support for Israel, a country that many people believed was deliberately suppressing the establishment of a Palestinian nation. A few of these angry people banded together to form terrorist groups, some of which were based on their extreme interpretation of their religion, Islam. At first, they limited their attacks to targets in the Middle East, but over the past 30 years, these targets have spread all over the world, as the extremists who carry them out try to heighten the exposure of their cause.

The September 11th terrorist attacks also provoked debate and discussion far beyond America's frontiers. Who committed these outrages? Why did they happen? As peaceful nations all over the world looked for terrorists to blame, governments made new allies and turned against former friends. Groups and leaders that had been funded and supported by the USA over the years were now seen as enemies and were held responsible for the September 11th attacks. These included Osama bin Laden, who the USA had supported in his fight against the Soviet Union; and Saddam Hussein, the leader of Iraq, whom the USA had supported in his war against Iran. America felt that it was justified in attacking these groups and the people who supported them – including other countries' governments – in the name of world security. Caught in the middle of this increasing tension was the United Nations, whose headquarters are in New York City itself. For over 50 years, this international organization had been responsible for overseeing peace throughout the world. Now it was caught between calls from the USA and its allies to take action against those countries held responsible, and other nations who felt that the USA was breaking international law in its hunt for terrorists and those it felt threatened world safety. With the wars in Afghanistan and Iraq it became clear that the old way of doing things had changed, and that the United States was not prepared to sit back and wait for another terrorist attack while the international community debated what to do next.

Osama bin Laden, head of al- Qaeda – the man said to be behind the terror attacks on the World Trade Center.

Nothing illustrates the global spread of American commercial influence better than Coca-Cola. This American product is consumed all over the world. Its logo has been translated into several different languages and alphabets (below).

F or nearly 50 years after the end of World War II, the world's two most powerful nations, the USA and the USSR, were enemies. They had different ways of life and different political ideals – the Soviet Union was a communist state; America was a free-market democracy. The two superpowers mistrusted and misunderstood each other, and their leaders quarrelled publicly. Both recruited smaller states to support their cause, and both wanted to spread their influence around the world. Although the United States and the USSR did not fight face-to-face, the tension between them was very strong. People called this period the 'Cold War'.

Alone – and powerful

In the 1950s, the United States and the USSR both built up massive nuclear weapons stocks in an arms race. However, by the 1980s, the Soviet Union's economy was so weak that the country could no longer afford to keep up. The people's appetite for communism in both the USSR and Eastern Europe was also waning, and by the end of the decade, a succession of countries had removed their communist leaders from power. Then in December 1991, the communist government in the USSR itself disbanded and the Soviet Union broke up. This left the United States as the world's only remaining superpower.

CAPITALISM

Capitalism is a 'free market' economic system in which the means of producing wealth, such as factories and shops, are owned by private individuals or corporations. In such a system, anyone can set up a business – if they have the money – and grow rich if it makes a profit. Businesses can compete with one another freely, with relatively few rules to govern their behaviour or protect purchasers. In free-market economies, taxes are often low, and state rules and welfare benefits are kept to a minimum. For anyone starting a business, however, the risks are high. If they fail, they might lose their home and their family might go hungry. But if they succeed, they could become very rich.

From cola to computers

American citizens enjoy one of the highest standard of living in the world and, for most of the 1990s, the American economy was booming. American products – from cola drinks, burgers and fries to TV soaps and serials – were in demand all over the world, from Australia to Zimbabwe. American technology – especially computer software and the Internet – revolutionized global communications, and influenced the style and content of news and entertainment media almost everywhere.

A takeover? Many people, in many lands, admired America's energy and enterprise. The US had become the richest, most powerful country in the world, but with the spread of American technology and culture, and with its dominant voice in international affairs, many people in other countries believed that the US had become too powerful, arrogant and insensitive to the concerns of the rest of the world. Some people watched in dismay as American products, movies,

games, fashions and foods from the world's only superpower spread across the globe, and feared that local cultures and traditions were being squeezed out. This made many people feel angry and insecure. Some wanted to rebel against what they saw as American values that were being imposed on them without their choice.

Americans have always been fiercely patriotic about their country (left).

The events of September 11th forced President George W Bush to get more involved in world affairs.

'The American destiny is what our fathers dreamed, a land of the free, and the home of the brave; but only the brave can be free. Science has made the dream of today's reality for all the earth if we have the courage and vision to build it. American democracy must furnish the engineers of world plenty — the builders of world peace and freedom.'

American writer Marian Le Sueur (1877–1954)

Wall Street (above) is the financial centre of the United States. Shares in corporations are bought and sold here on the New York Stock Exchange, the 'engine room' of American commercial wealth and power.

Money talks!

As the most powerful economy in the world, America is also home to many multinational companies, such as McDonald's and Coca Cola, which sell their products and extend their operations all over the world. These companies take advantages of the market system, feeling free to produce goods as cheaply as possible – for example, by locating their factories in countries where wages are low, and selling what they produce as higher prices in wealthier nations. American governments promoted new institutions, such as the World Trade Organization, which encouraged the growth of free trade around the world. This led to bitter controversy. Supporters of free trade claim that it helps poor countries to develop their economies, create jobs and improve standards of living. But critics argue that this system exploits those poor countries and takes advantage of their powerlessness. They say the system forces them to adopt a wealthy nation's materialistic beliefs and values.

FOUR *freedoms*

In 1941, American President Franklin D Roosevelt proclaimed that, in his view, all humanity should be entitled to 'Four Freedoms', already enjoyed by the citizens of the USA. These were:

- *freedom of speech;*
- *freedom of worship;*
- *freedom of expression;*
- *freedom from want and fear.*

Religious freedom

As well as supporting free trade, America also proclaimed other freedoms, which it believed all people should enjoy. These include free speech - the right to express opinions without fear of punishment – and also freedom of religion. Although many Americans are deeply religious, the USA is a secular (non-religious) state by law. The right to hold any religious faith – or none – was guaranteed by the US Constitution. This famous statement of the rules by which the nation is governed was drawn up by America's founding fathers (leading statesmen) in 1787.

The American Way

Although Americans often criticised their national and local governments, most believed that these freedoms made their country the best in the world. The millions of immigrants who flocked to America in the 19th and 20th centuries to seek a better future were proud to follow 'the American way of life'. Americans honoured democratic institutions such as the House of Representatives and the Senate, they upheld law and order, they admired their nation's economic strength and military power, and they saluted national symbols such as the American flag.

Disapproval

American ideals of freedom and democracy were shared by many people in Western Europe, and also by people in countries that had once been under communist control. But these ideals did not please everybody. Some powerful nations, including China, admired economic freedom but did not support the same level of freedom. And many Muslim nations, including Saudi Arabia and Iran, feared that Western ways could be dangerous and corrupt their societies. By the late 20th century, this dislike of Western society in many parts of the Muslim world mingled with ancient religious and political tensions to create an explosive mixture of fear and distrust.

'The Westerners have lost the vision of heaven,

All they care about is food and possessions,

But the pure soul is untouched by greed and desire.

Communism is only concerned with physical needs…

It is based on equality of greed…

But true brotherhood belongs to the heart,

It does not need material things.

Capitalism is also greedy for goods,

It had no heart or soul…'

From 'Javidnama' written by Muslim poet Muhammad Iqbal, in 1932.

The Statue of Liberty (left) stands proudly before New York City, USA, as a powerful symbol of American freedom and democracy.

A map of Israel, showing the disputed West Bank territory.

WEST BANK

The Middle East

One section of the Middle East is often called 'the Holy Land'. Today, it is divided among Syria, Israel, Jordan and the disputed Palestinian territories. The Holy Land is sacred to people from three of the world's great faiths — Judaism, Christianity and Islam. Its most important city, Jerusalem, contains holy sites visited by pilgrims from all these faiths.

Promised Land

For Jews, the Holy Land is where their ancestors settled after Moses led them out of Egypt in about 1,200 BC. They believe the land was promised to them by God. For Christians, the Holy Land is sacred because Jesus Christ lived and preached there. They believe that he rose from the dead, after he was executed in about AD 30.

God's last messenger

Muslims honour Moses and Jesus Christ as prophets — messengers sent by God to show people the right way to live. But they believe that the Prophet Muhammad, who lived in the years AD 570–632, was God's greatest messenger — and also his last. Like Jews and Christians, they respect the land where Moses and Jesus once preached. But they feel special reverence for the Arabian holy cities of Mecca, where the Prophet Muhammad spent most of his life, and Medina, where he is buried. They also honour other holy places in neighbouring Middle Eastern countries, including Iraq and Iran.

THE DOME *of the Rock*

This Muslim holy place in Jerusalem was built around AD 691. Muslims believe that the Prophet Muhammad made a miraculous journey to heaven from a rocky outcrop here, and returned to teach people how to pray. The site on which the dome stands is called the Noble Sanctuary by Muslims but it is also holy to the Jews, who call it Temple Mount. They believe it was where God commanded Abraham to sacrifice his son Isaac. It was also the place where the Jewish King Solomon built the first great Jewish temple to worship God.

Disputed territory The Holy Land has always been disputed territory. In ancient times, it was home to several warring peoples including Jews, Philistines and Samaritans. It was conquered by the Romans in AD 6, and by Muslims in AD 634. From 1098 until 1197, it was ruled by Christian soldiers during the Crusades. After being re-taken by Muslim armies, it became part of the Muslim Ottoman Empire in 1516 and remained under Turkish rule, along with most of Arabia and Iraq, until 1917. That year, the Ottoman Empire's power collapsed after it was defeated in World War I. Since then, many parts of the Middle East, including the Holy Land, have been constantly threatened by upheaval or war.

Sand and oil

As well as being 'holy', the lands of the Middle East are remarkable in another way. In the late 19th and early 20th centuries, geologists discovered that the rocks deep under the stony desert soil contained vast reserves of valuable oil.

Almost one-half of all the world's known oil deposits belong to Iran, Iraq, Saudi Arabia, Kuwait and neighbouring smaller countries. This new oil wealth gave Middle Eastern countries enormous power — but it also made them vulnerable to attack.

This Saudi refinery (left) processes oil from the Persian Gulf. Wealth from oil has transformed a previously impoverished area into a region of wealthy, high-tech kingdoms.

BLACK *gold*

Oil is an extraordinarily valuable commodity. It is often called 'black gold'. Oil is considered a nonrenewable source, which means that once we have used the supplies that currently exist, people will not be able to create more. If oil supplies were cut off, everyday life in all industrialised countries would be impossible. Cars, aircraft, trains, heating systems and many other machines all rely on oil-based fuels. Many plastics, detergents, cosmetics, dyes, food flavourings and lubricants are also made from oil.

An Afghan mujahedin (Muslim fighter) defends his faith after his country is invaded by the USSR in 1979 (below).

Independence

In 1920, after the collapse of the Ottoman Empire, an organization called the League of Nations gave Britain and France special authority to govern large areas of the Middle East. But many Middle Eastern peoples demanded the right to become independent nations so that they could govern themselves and make their own laws. In several of the new countries, these laws were based on religion.

Saudi Arabia

In Arabia, for example, demands for independence were led by Abd al-Aziz Ibn Saud (1880–1953). He supported the strict Wahhabi religious reform movement, which aimed to purify Islam. With the help of Wahhabi brotherhoods, he helped make Arabia an independent state in 1932. Ibn Saud became king, and declared that Arabia should be ruled according to shariyah (Muslim holy law, based on the Muslim holy book, the Qur'an), and by royal decree. He also renamed the state after his family. After oil was discovered in Saudi Arabia in 1938, Ibn Saud became even more powerful.

Iraq and Iran

In neighbouring Iraq and Iran, which also had rich reserves of oil, campaigners won independence in 1921 and 1925. But for many years afterwards, European and later, American governments interfered in politics in this region, backing some leaders and working to weaken others. Western oil companies did not want to lose control of profitable oil reserves and refineries, and Western governments wanted to stop other powerful nations from getting control of Middle Eastern oil. In 1979, anti-western Muslim leaders seized power in Iran, launching a strict 'Islamic Revolution'.

Israel

Jewish people also demanded a homeland of their own. The First Zionist Congress (international meeting of Jewish campaigners) was held in 1897. In 1917, British Foreign Secretary Arthur Balfour issued a statement supporting a new Jewish state in Palestine, so long as 'nothing shall be done which may prejudice the civil and religious rites of existing non-Jewish communities'. By 1939, half a million Jewish people had settled in

the CRUSADES

The Crusades were a series of seven wars fought to win control of the Holy Land between the 11th and 14th centuries. Crusaders (knights and foot-soldiers) were inspired by preachers who feared that Islam would soon spread westwards into Europe. Soldiers from many Muslim lands, from Turkey to Egypt, fought to defend their Islamic faith and their Muslim lifestyle and laws. The fighting was brutal, and both sides committed many atrocities. The Crusades left a heritage of bitterness and misunderstanding that still continues today.

PURE *Islam*

Arab religious reformer Muhammad Ibn Abd al-Wahhab (died 1791) believed that many Muslim customs that had been adopted and added over the centuries, such as honouring saints at shrines, were damaging to Islam. He also condemned western ideas and values. He called for a return to 'pure', strict Muslim belief and worship, which focused on 'tawhid' – the unity and oneness of God. Wahhabi ideas helped establish the Kingdom of Saudi Arabia, and still guide its government policies today.

Radical Muslims in Pakistan carry images of their hero Osama bin Laden after the September 11th attacks (above). The secular government of Pakistan walked a tightrope between its Western allies and interests, and its fundamentalist Muslim citizens.

Palestine, and there were serious tensions between Arabs (both Christian and Muslim) and Jews. In 1947, the UN declared that Palestine should be divided into Jewish and Arab states, and the nation of Israel was born. It had a western-style secular constitution, but Jewish religious laws and traditions played an important part in shaping its citizens' lives.

Holy laws, holy wars

Religious laws have pleased many devout citizens within Jewish, Christian and Muslim lands around the world. But, when neighbouring countries become involved in a dispute, religious laws can often make a conflict worse. From the time of the Crusades onwards, soldiers from different faiths have justified many appalling acts of violence in the Middle East by claiming that they were fighting 'a holy war'. With both sides believing that their cause had God's blessing, they felt free to indulge their hatred, prejudice and intolerance towards others of a different faith or race.

Terrorism has a long history. The word was first used in 1793, during a period of the French Revolution that became known as 'The Terror'. At that time, republicans with extreme views used guillotines to execute the French king and queen, as well as thousands of members of the French nobility and people who were suspected of sympathizing with them. Since then, there have been terrorist attacks in many parts of the world. Typical terror tactics include assassination, hostage-taking, hijacking and mass-murder.

The Kikuyu people in Kenya (above) have always been amongst the poorest in the country. In the 1950s, the Mau Mau organization, which included extreme members of the tribe, launched a series of attacks to try and force the Europeans out of Kenya.

Bombs and bullets

In Russia during the 1870s and 1880s, a radical group known as 'Narodnaya Volya' ('The People's Will') threw bombs at members of the Russian government, and shot dead the Russian monarch Tsar Alexander II in 1881. They hoped that once their hated leaders had been overthrown, ordinary people would revolt and create a new communist state.

Surprise attacks

In 1950s Kenya, the secret Mau Mau organization was formed by radical members of the Kikuyu tribe to fight against Europeans who had settled in their country. They made night-time attacks on remote villages and farms. Later, the Mau Mau became anti-Christian as well as anti-European, and very violent. They killed 50 white people, and more than 11,000 Africans. As a result of Mau Mau activities, many Europeans left Kenya when the nation became independent from Britain in 1963.

WHO *is a terrorist?*

Some experts say that a terrorist is anyone who uses terror to get what they want, even if they have good reasons to justify their actions. Other experts argue that people who normally campaign by peaceful, lawful means may occasionally use terror to fight for their rights or to defend themselves from powerful enemies. Their behaviour is terrible and terrifying, but it does not make them terrorists.

Suicide bombers

In Sri Lanka during the 1970s, members of the Tamil ethnic minority protested against their treatment by the majority Sinhalese, and demanded an independent Tamil homeland in northern Sri Lanka. While many worked peacefully, others set up camps to train terrorists, who were known as the 'Tamil Tigers'. Suicide bombers were sent to buses, trains, shops and market places. They aimed to kill the maximum number of people, including women and children. This tactic caused widespread panic.

Hijacking and publicity

In the Middle East in the 1970s, Palestinian terrorists hijacked several large aircraft. They set the passengers free, unharmed, then blew the planes up on the ground. They wanted to win the maximum publicity for their cause – ending Israeli occupation of the West Bank area, and setting up an independent Palestinian state. In 1976, a Muslim leader named Sheikh Yassin Ahmad founded Hamas, a Palestinian resistance movement. It was originally non-militant, but soon began to use increasingly violent means, including suicide bombings and assassinations.

'Millions of innocent children are being killed as I speak. They are being killed in Iraq without committing any sins... In these days, Israeli tanks infest Palestine... and we don't hear anyone raising his voice or moving a limb.'

Comment from Osama bin Laden, prior to the terrorist attacks in the USA.

Outside the state!

Terrorism is not like ordinary warfare. Terrorist fighters are not recruited, trained or commanded by lawful governments. And they do not obey any of the normal 'rules of war' agreed by governments to protect innocent civilians, prisoners of war and medical teams on both sides. There are many terrorist groups operating all over the world today.

Basque Region

Portugal

Spain

This map (above) shows the Basque region. The territory lies in both France and Spain.

Londonderry
Belfast
Northern Ireland
Dublin
Ireland
Cork

This map (above) shows the division of Ireland into north and south.

A masked terrorist throws a Molotov cocktail in West Belfast, Northern Ireland. The situation in the province is complicated by a religious divide, as well as a political one.

Freedom fighters

In 1990s Spain, a group known as ETA (the Basque Freedom and Liberty organisation) recruited members from the Basque area of northern Spain and south-west France. The Basque people have a unique culture and form an ethnic minority in the two countries. They used car bombings and murders to terrorize cities and towns. ETA claimed to be fighting for freedom, and the right for a separate Basque state.

They said that violence was necessary to make the Spanish and French governments listen to their demands.

Mighty enemies

In Chechnya, a region in the south-west of the Russian Federation, rebels demanded independence from Russia during the 1990s. They had no chance of winning an ordinary war against this mighty enemy, but realised that with terrorist tactics they could achieve maximum impact using the smallest number of fighters and weapons they had, a tactic known as guerrilla warfare. The more the Russians fight back, the more determined the Chechen rebels have become — even though this has caused their own people dreadful suffering.

Hopes of Heaven

On the Palestinian West Bank during the 1990s, would-be suicide bombers felt hopeless, desperate and very angry. Like many volunteers who join terrorist organizations, they believed they had to 'do something', and sacrificed their lives in the hope of winning a better future for their people. They also believed that their actions would win them a blissful reward in heaven — although many Muslim scholars say that this hope was based on mistaken religious ideas.

Ideology During the 1980s and 1990s, in countries as far apart as Peru and Nepal, hundreds of police, government officials, doctors and teachers were killed by Maoist terrorists. These men and women followed the teachings of the former Chinese communist leader Mao Zedong. Mao's writings urge workers to take part in a 'permanent revolution', in which all members of the ruling class will be overthrown, and ordinary people will control all political and economic power. The terrorists followed the example of Mao himself, who was extremely ruthless and believed that his deeds were justified by his goal.

Intimidation

In the 1990s, Northern Ireland's two warring factions, the Nationalists (Irish republicans) and the Loyalists (pro-British), each had armed gangs and terrorist organisations. These two groups often attacked members of their own communities who befriended people from 'enemy' backgrounds, or who worked to bring about peace. Both sides claimed that this was necessary for 'security' reasons. Because these groups act outside the law, many terrorists live in fear of being betrayed. So they use brutal tactics to force people to help them, or to keep quiet. As a result, revenge killings and bloody feuds can be common.

Fighting between guerrillas and Russian soldiers in Chechnya (above) has been fierce, with atrocities committed by both sides.

Al-Qaeda Although there have been terrorist attacks throughout the world, many of the worst ones have taken place in the Middle East. Many dangerous and determined terrorist organizations are based in the region. These included a group known as 'al-Qaeda' ('The Base'). Founded in 1989 by Saudi Arabian millionaire Osama bin Laden, al-Qaeda's aim is to unite all Muslims and set up a world Islamic government. Today, it has members all over the world who support its terrorist activities.

CRIMINAL *involvement*

Terrorists often work alongside criminals, for example in the South American nation of Colombia. They both share a common enemy – the lawful government of the land where they live – and use violence to get what they want. Criminals supply weapons and ammunition to terrorists. In return, terrorists help criminals to operate illegal businesses, especially the profitable cocaine trade.

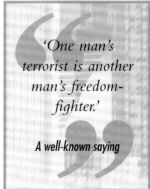

'One man's terrorist is another man's freedom-fighter.'

A well-known saying

OSAMA *bin Laden*

Osama bin Laden was born in Saudi Arabia to a wealthy family in 1957. During the 1980s he fought against the Soviet invaders in Afghanistan – with support from the USA. After Soviet troops left Afghanistan, he returned to Saudi Arabia, where he campaigned against the Saudi government and against the presence of foreigners until he was expelled in 1991. In 1996, he returned to Afghanistan where the fundamentalist Muslim Taliban were in power. There, he used his wealth to recruit and train terrorists, and to pay for their terrorist operations.

Osama bin Laden (right) began his terrorist career because of two issues that outraged him more than any others. These were the presence of non-Muslim western foreigners in Saudi Arabia, the birthplace of the prophet Muhammad, and the West's refusal to allow the Palestinians an independent homeland.

Muslim anger

After Israel became an independent state in 1948, Palestinians looked forward to a homeland of their own. But Israeli governments would not agree to this. This led to wars between Israel and groups of Arab nations, including Egypt, Syria, Transjordan (later Jordan), Lebanon, Iraq and Saudi Arabia. In 1967, Israel occupied the West Bank region and the Gaza Strip, where Arabs lived. In 1987, Palestinian terrorists launched an unsuccessful intifada (uprising) in an attempt to win the land back. Arabs in many Middle Eastern lands and Muslims from all over the world offered their support to the cause.

Fundamentalism

After the creation of Israel and with the dominance of Western culture, Muslim reformers began to attract more supporters. Their radical message, which called for a return to pure Islamic beliefs and for shariyah (Muslim holy law), found many sympathetic ears. Some of these supporters disliked Western secular beliefs. Others were inspired by the Iranian Islamic Revolution of 1979, or wanted to defend Muslim countries against Israel, the USA or Soviet Russia.

Muslim Jihad

During the Cold War, the USA and the Soviet Union both wanted to control the poor, undeveloped country of Afghanistan. In 1979, Soviet troops invaded the country. Afghan 'mujahedin' (Muslim guerrilla fighters) fought back ferociously, claiming that their struggle was a 'jihad' ('holy war'). Osama bin Laden sent Muslim volunteers from many lands, who had been trained

JIHAD *against America*

In 1998, al-Qaeda issued a statement. In it, members claimed to represent 'the World Islamic Front for Jihad Against Jews and Crusaders'. They declared that it was 'the duty of all Muslims to kill US citizens – civilians or military – and their allies everywhere'. In Arabic, 'jihad' means 'holy war'. But it also means many other kinds of struggle, such as trying hard to be good, to work well or to live an honest, useful life.

in terror tactics, to help them. This new terrorist group was the organization that became al-Qaeda. Ironically, bin Laden was supported in his struggle against the USSR by the USA.

Muslim impact

Members of al-Qaeda soon became active in many other parts of the world, and attracted more recruits. In 1993, they shot down American army helicopters in the African nation of Somalia, and were thought to be behind a small attack on the World Trade Center in New York in the same year. In 1994 and 1995, they plotted to kill the Pope and President Bill Clinton in the Philippines. In 1998, they bombed American embassies in Kenya and Tanzania and in 1999, they planned to kill American and Israeli tourists in Jordan. In 2000, they attacked the US Navy ship USS *Cole* in Yemen. Then members began to plan the most ambitious attack yet - a new assault on the World Trade Center. Most of the men who carried out this attack were chosen for their aviation knowledge. Several of the hijackers had studied aircraft construction in Germany during the 1990s, while others took flying lessons in Europe and in the US prior to the attacks. All managed to enter the US legally on temporary tourist, business and student visas.

THE CRITICAL MOMENT  *September 11th*

It was the height of the rush hour on a beautiful September morning in New York. Thousands of men and women were arriving at offices throughout the city. They included staff from the many international businesses whose offices were in the World Trade Center – two tall towers, 110 storeys high, that stood as proud symbols of enterprise and capitalism in a country that considered itself the leader of the free world. On a normal weekday, more than 50,000 people worked in the towers.

08:28

FIRST HIJACK

American Airlines Flight 11, a Boeing 767 jet bound for Los Angeles, took off from Logan Airport, Boston. At 8.28 am, a group of four hijackers, led by a man named Mohammad Atta, took over the cockpit. They

Mohammad Atta, leader of the Flight 11 hijackers.

were armed with knives. On the ground, air-control staff overheard them say, 'Don't do anything foolish. You are not going to get hurt. We have other planes.'

FLIGHT 175   **08:30**

At about 8.30 am, passengers and crew on board a second aircraft, United Airlines Flight 175, were overpowered by five more hijackers armed with knives. Their flight had left Boston for Los Angeles at 7.58 am, with 65 people on board. In their struggle to take control of the plane, the hijackers stabbed one of the cabin crew. Bravely, a woman flight attendant managed to get a warning message to air traffic control on the ground.

United Airlines Flight 175.

Officials at NORAD keep watch over American skies.

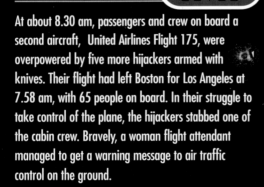

NORAD   **08:40**

At 8.40 am, the US Federal Aviation Administration sent out alerts to the North American Aerospace Defence Command (NORAD – the military organization that guards the skies over Canada and the USA). It warned of not one, but two hijacks – American Airlines Flight 11 and United Airlines Flight 175 also heading for Los Angeles. NORAD scrambled (urgently launched) two F-15 jet fighters from Otis Air National Guard Base in Falmouth, Massachusetts.

DISASTER STRIKES

`08:48`

Instead of heading west from Boston towards its planned destination, American Airlines Flight 11 changed direction, and flew south towards New York. Travelling at about 800 km/h (500 mph), it crashed into the North Tower of the World Trade Center, between the 95th and 103rd floors. The impact killed all 92 people on board – passengers, crew and four hijackers – and hundreds of people in the North Tower. These included about 80 chefs, waiters and kitchen staff who worked at the 'Windows on the World restaurant on the 106th floor. People in America and all over the world watched in disbelief as live reports began to appear on television screens showing black smoke billowing from the North Tower of the World Trade Center in New York City. Had there been some sort of dreadful accident?

The first plane plunges into the North Tower.

VIEWS *from the ground*

'At 08:48, as I was sitting in my chair, I felt a tremendous jolt. My office chair rolled in one direction and then the opposite direction. During the sway, I could hear the grinding of concrete and steel. Burning metal pieces and tonnes of paper were flying outside the south windows and falling to the ground below.

Several people just stared out the windows, completely shocked at what they were seeing. I really thought the building was going to fall down right then and there.'

A World Trade Center worker remembers
Quoted on BBC news

THE CRITICAL MOMENT

09:03

DISASTER AT THE SOUTH TOWER

As they looked through their viewfinders, camera crews were appalled to see a second aircraft heading for the World Trade Center. It was Flight 175. At 9.03 am, together with millions of TV viewers and workers in nearby buildings, they watched in horror as the plane crashed into the South Tower. It hit the building at about the level of the 80th floor, forcing a massive cloud of dust, smoke and vaporised aircraft fuel out of the far side.

The second plane crashes into the South Tower setting it on fire.

President Bush was informed immediately of the attack.

THE PRESIDENT IS TOLD   09:10

At first, most onlookers thought the World Trade Center crash was a tragic accident, or perhaps the work of a lone madman. But some American government officials were suspicious. They immediately gave the news to President Bush, who was visiting a school in Florida and reading to children in a classroom. By 9.20 am, the FBI had begun investigations into a possible terrorist attack.

09:29

FIRST FIREFIGHTERS

By 9.29 am, the first police officers, firefighters and ambulance crews had arrived at the World Trade Center. Bravely, they went inside as office workers from the lower floors of both towers began to leave the building. In Florida, a grim-faced President Bush told reporters, 'We have had a national tragedy'.

VIEWS *from the ground*

'We saw both towers on fire. Both towers had similar, charred, massive holes in their sides, and bright red flames were coming out of the damaged areas. It was unbelievable.

By this time, my colleagues were crying and looking at the towers in disbelief. They had their arms around one another. We walked to the corner of Fulton and Broadway, and

I saw something horrible. I recognized a piece of a jet airliner's front landing gear.

It was on the street, underneath what looked like a large pool of blood. There was so much blood on the street.'

A World Trade Center worker, who escaped from the building, remembers, Quoted on BBC news

A New York firefighter, blackened by the smoke and dust of the burning buildings, helps people to safety.

09:40

HEART OF THE GOVERNMENT

At 9.40 am, a third aircraft (American Airlines Flight 77 bound from Washington DC to Los Angeles) crashed into the Pentagon, just outside Washington DC – one of the most secure buildings in the world. Built to an extraordinary five-sided design, the fortress-like Pentagon is the command centre of the American armed forces. As Flight 77 came down it exploded, creating a massive fireball and causing five floors of the Pentagon building to collapse. All 64 people on board Flight 77, including the five hijackers, were killed. About 190 Pentagon staff also died.

The ruins of the Pentagon after it was struck by Flight 77.

The White House, home of the American president.

WASHINGTON IN DANGER

09:45

By 9.45 am, security experts feared that the president's life and the lives of his staff were in danger. Key buildings in Washington DC including the White House (home and headquarters of the American president) and the Capitol (which houses government and law offices) were evacuated. Just five minutes later, all American airports were closed and all airborne commercial flights were ordered to land as soon as possible. Such an order had never been given before.

THE PITTSBURGH PLANE

At 10.04 am, yet another plane crash was reported. This time, the aircraft landed in a field about 130 km (81 miles) south-east of Pittsburgh — an industrial city in the American mid-west. The crashed plane was United Airlines Flight 93, heading to San Francisco from Newark, New Jersey. It had 45 passengers, including four hijackers armed with knives and a box they said contained a bomb. At first, no-one connected this crash with the other terrorist attacks. But then they realised that the passengers had forced the hijackers to steer the aircraft away from its intended target. This was probably an important government building in Washington DC — maybe even the White House itself!

VIEWS *from the ground*

'I want to reassure the American people that the full resources of the federal government are working to assist local authorities to save lives and help the victims of these attacks... The resolve of our great nation is being tested. But make no mistake: we will show the world that we will pass this test.'

Emergency statement by President Bush 12.39 pm, September 11, 2001

The remains of Flight 93 lie in a Pittsburgh field.

When the Towers collapsed, the streets were filled with acrid smoke.

COLLAPSE

Back in New York, there were scenes of almost unimaginable horror. Workers on the lower floors of the North and South Towers of the World Trade Center struggled to find their way down through blinding, burning clouds of poisonous smoke. Some lost their way in the dark and became trapped, never to escape alive. Others perished, gasping and choking, as heat and fumes scorched their lungs. Higher up in the towers, above the impact zone, men and women jumped to their deaths from office windows, rather than wait for the fire to reach them and be burned alive. Then suddenly, with an appalling rumble, the South Tower collapsed. Like many modern office buildings, the World Trade Center had been built around a framework of steel. But the aircraft crash had soaked it with more than 90,000 litres (23,700 gallons) of flammable aircraft fuel. As this blazed furiously, temperatures around the impact zone soared to more than 800°C (1,450°F). The steel frame softened, causing the concrete floors and walls it once supported to collapse. Hundreds of office workers — together with the police, firefighters and ambulance crews who were helping them to leave the building — were crushed under 100,000 tonnes of rubble as the South Tower fell down.

THE NORTH TOWER CRUMBLES

`10:29`

The deadly roar of the south tower collapsing had hardly died away when the north tower also crumpled and crashed to the ground. People outside the World Trade Center ran for their lives as a massive cloud of dust and smoke swirled around the ruins, and shards of glass and slabs of concrete rained down on them from the sky. Hundreds more World Trade Center workers and emergency personnel were killed. In less than two hours, the proudest symbol of American free trade had been destroyed.

The North Tower lies in ruins.

Powerfull fighter planes roared over Washington DC and New York after the attacks.

`13:20`

PROTECTING THE PRESIDENT

For safety reasons, President Bush was flown to the isolated Offutt Air Force Base in rural Nebraska at 1.20 pm. Minutes later, American army and navy commanders sent seven warships to guard the east coast of America, and ordered extra fighter planes to patrol the skies above Washington DC and New York. At 1.50 pm, the Mayor of Washington DC declared a state of emergency in the capital, giving police and soldiers sweeping powers to act against suspected terrorists.

14:48 Although police officers, firefighters and ambulance crew had just seen many of their colleagues killed, they bravely began a search through the rubble of the collapsed World Trade Center. But it soon became clear that very few people in, or close to, either tower had survived. Searchers found just five survivors in the first 24 hours. Long before then, New Yorkers were beginning to realise the scale of the tragedy that had hit them. In an emotional statement, four hours after the first tower collapsed, the city's mayor, Rudolph Giuliani, declared that the death toll might be 'more than any of us can bear'. To many people it seemed as if doomsday — the end of the world — had come.

Mayor Rudolph Giuliani prepares to deliver his speech.

At 8.30 pm on September 11, 2001, President Bush made an official TV broadcast to the American nation. In it, he spoke of the deep shock at the attack, but how the people of America would stand together and beat the terrorists.

President Bush gives a sombre address to the Nation.

BROADCAST *to the nation*

'Today, our fellow citizens, our way of life, our very freedom came under attack in a series of deliberate and deadly terrorist acts. These acts of mass murder were intended to frighten our nation into chaos and retreat. But they have failed. Terrorist attacks can shake the foundations of our biggest buildings, but they cannot touch the foundation of America.'

President Bush made an official TV broadcast to the American nation

As the smoke and dust slowly settled over the crumpled remains of the World Trade Center, the citizens of New York were left with a gash in their famous skyline and a hole in their hearts. The devastated site soon became known as 'Ground Zero'. President Bush summed up their thoughts: 'None of us will ever forget this day'.

For weeks after the event, heart-breaking pleas for help, such as this one (below), were posted around Ground Zero by people hoping that their loved ones had somehow survived the calamity.

We Need Your Help

Giovanna "Gennie" Gambale

27 years old 5'6"
Brown hair, brown eyes
Last seen on 102nd fl of World Trade Center I
(E-Speed/Cantor-Fitzgerald)
Call with any information 718-624-0465

A terrible toll In the days following the terrorist attacks, emergency workers continued to search through the rubble, but they found very few survivors. Eventually, the final toll of all those killed by the terrorists in New York and Washington DC was published. It totalled more than 3,000 innocent civilians. Many thousands more men, women and children were mourning loved ones, colleagues and neighbours who had lost their lives in the tragedy.

In ruins New Yorkers also suffered whenever they saw the ruined buildings at Ground Zero. As engineers and construction workers laboured to clear rubble and make the site safe, one volunteer rescuer said in disbelief, 'I never thought I'd see the World Trade Center pass me by in a dump truck'. Some experts feared that shock waves from the collapsing towers may have destabilized the surrounding ground, and that the Hudson River might flood the whole business district of New York. Fortunately, their predictions did not come true, but many buildings close to Ground Zero proved to be seriously damaged, and one collapsed.

America's finest There was, however, just a little good news among the reports of death and destruction. As the survivors recalled their

CASUALTY *statistics*

World Trade Center deaths	2,792	Deaths on aircraft	261
World Trade Center injured	2,261	Firefighter deaths	343
Pentagon deaths	124	Police deaths	75
Pentagon injured	76		

experiences, they told stories of great bravery and heroism by members of the emergency services, especially the firefighters. They remembered how crewmen and women had courageously entered the burning towers to lead office workers to safety, even though firefighters knew how likely the buildings were to collapse. Ambulance crews, too, had rushed towards the inferno as others were running away in fear of their lives. These brave people were hailed as 'America's finest'. Mayor Giuliani was also praised for his inspiring leadership, and many world leaders sent messages of sympathy and support.

A blow to business

The terrorists' choice of the World Trade Center as their target was deliberate. They hoped that confidence in American business would collapse, along with the towers. This did not happen, but for

CONDEMNATION *of the attacks*

'Yesterday was indeed a dark day in our history, an appalling offence against peace, a terrible assault against human dignity.'
– Pope John Paul II

'This is a war between good and evil and between humanity and the bloodthirsty...'
– Prime Minister Ariel Sharon of Israel

'We were completely shocked... It's unbelievable, unbelievable, unbelievable...'
– President Yasser Arafat of Palestine

'I condemn them utterly...'
– United Nations Secretary General Kofi Annan

the first time in more than 50 years, people did start to question America's economic power. Before the attack, this had seemed unshakeable. Afterwards, however, American customers and investors became very cautious, and the US economy slowed down.

President George W Bush addresses members of the emergency services before the rubble and wreckage of Ground Zero.

Most practising Muslims were as outraged by the terrorist attacks as everyone else, but many were treated with deep suspicion after the attacks.

Changing climate

Before the attacks, Americans prided themselves on their free and easy ways. These ranged from welcoming strangers with few questions asked to the right for anyone to own a gun. The American way of life seemed safe and secure behind the nation's natural frontiers of deserts, mountains and oceans, and its armed forces were the strongest in the world.

What went wrong?

After the attacks, however, America no longer seemed such a safe place to live. And, once the shock of the terrorist attacks had passed, people began to ask questions – in particular, why had there been no warning? The two main intelligence organisations, the CIA (Central Intelligence Agency) and the FBI (Federal Bureau of Investigation), were accused of not connecting the dots--failing to piece together all the clues that their intelligence agents had gathered, such as the suspicious behavior of the hijackers at flight-training schools in the US in the months before the attacks. To prevent similar failures in future, all American security personnel throughout the world were put on high alert. President Bush vowed to find those responsible for the September 11th attacks and bring them to justice, promising an international 'crusade [to] rid the world of evil-doers'.

Homeland security

The US government also set up a new department, responsible for 'homeland security'. Controversially, police arrested hundreds of young (mostly Muslim) men and accused them of entering the US illegally--even though most of the Sept. 11 hijackers had managed to get into the country legally." . Using airports to travel abroad and within the USA became much more difficult, as all passengers at airports now had to pass through much tighter security checks. Even seemingly 'innocent' items, such as nail scissors and metal cutlery, were banned from being taken on board planes. Delays caused by these travel checks and the fear of further terrorist attacks caused a sharp drop in the number of tourists visiting America. Many Americans also cancelled their plans to travel abroad, whether on holiday or for business.

Deadly packages
This climate of fear worsened after packets of a mysterious white powder were posted to government offices and media companies in several American cities. The packets contained the spores (tiny seeds) of the deadly germ, anthrax. Panic spread across the country, and hospitals stockpiled large amounts of antibiotics, ready to use as an antidote. Today, the police think the anthrax packets were probably the work of a lone criminal, but no-one knows for sure.

THE PRESIDENT'S response

'We are a different country than we were on September 10, sadder and less innocent, stronger and more united. And in the face of ongoing threats, determined and courageous. Our nation faces a threat to our freedoms, and the stakes could not be higher. We are the target of enemies who boast that they want to kill, kill all Americans, kill all Jews and kill all Christians...'

President Bush, speaking two months after the attacks

Germ warfare?
Intelligence experts also warned that al-Qaeda terrorists, or the governments that supported them, might one day launch a germ warfare attack against America. Taking no chances, the American government ordered enough smallpox vaccine to protect every single citizen. Fears deepened after Osama bin Laden appeared on a videotape, making fresh threats against America and its people.

'The terrorists seem to have succeeded much beyond their own expectations... I can't think of anything that has disrupted government so much since the Civil War.'

James Thurber, a professor of American government on the disruption to the American postal service during the anthrax scare, October–November 2001

Throughout the anthrax crisis, US customs remained on heightened alert for any suspect material entering the country.

PORT AUTHORITY POLICE

*J*ust *two days after the attacks, American Secretary of State Colin Powell accused Osama bin Laden of masterminding the terrorist attacks on the World Trade Center. The US government believed that al-Qaeda was the only group who had the capacity to pull of such an attack. The world's attention focused on Afghanistan, where intelligence experts believed Osama bin Laden was hiding.*

Many Taliban recruits (below) were uprooted young men from refugee camps on the border between Pakistan and Afghanistan. Poor and angry, they found the Taliban's radical version of Islam appealing.

The Taliban
Since 1989, when Soviet troops left the country, there had been no strong, settled government in Afghanistan. Instead, the country was controlled by rival warlords.

In 1996, a group of young Islamic militants, calling themselves 'the Taliban' ('God's Students') seized control of most of the country, forcing government ministers to flee. Founded in 1994 by Afghan Muslim religious teacher Mullah Mohammad Omar, the Taliban at first fought lawlessness and corruption. The group attracted many recruits among poor, unemployed young men from villages in Afghanistan and from the large refugee camps across the border in Pakistan — where many Afghan families had lived in crowded, miserable conditions since the USSR invaded their country in 1979. Taliban recruits were appalled by the civil wars that were ruining their country. They also hated the growing popularity among wealthy Afghan people of western entertainment, fashions and secular, scientific ideas.

A CONTINUING *problem*

For the Americans, winning the Afghan war was easy. But it has proved much more difficult to achieve a satisfactory peace. Although the country is being stabilized by the ISAF (the International Security Assistance Force), fighting among rival warlords continues, especially in the north. Afghan people are still desperately poor, and their situation has been made worse by severe droughts. The new government controls Kabul, the capital, but not much of the rest of the country. Money and expert help, promised by the international community, has been tragically slow to reach the people who need it.

Strict Islam
By 1999, Taliban forces numbered about 30,000 militia (volunteer soldiers). They also had tanks and aircraft captured

American troops set off for Kabul, the capital of Afghanistan (top), and British troops blow up enemy missiles in the country (below).

from Afghan warlords. Troops of the Taliban patrolled Afghan villages and towns, forcing their own strict view of Islam on all citizens. They closed schools, banned music and dancing, and forbade all women (even doctors and nurses) from working outside the home. Hoping to spread their own fundamentalist views, they supported Muslim terrorist groups in other countries, including al-Qaeda.

Ready for war
On September 14th, 2001, the US government mobilised 50,000 reserve troops, and ordered aircraft and warships to bases within easy reach of Afghanistan. President Bush called for the Taliban to hand over Osama bin Laden 'dead or alive', and threatened dire revenge if they failed to co-operate. The Taliban refused. Instead, they asked Muslims all over the world to begin a 'holy war' against America.

Attack and surrender
On October 7th, 2001, the Americans attacked Afghanistan with bombs and heavy artillery. Faced with this massive firepower, the Taliban had no chance. Its members were killed or went into hiding. By December, a new civilian government backed by America and most of the international community was given the daunting task of reuniting and rebuilding poverty-stricken, war-torn Afghanistan.

'By destroying camps and disrupting communications, we'll make it more difficult for the terror network to train new recruits and co-ordinate their evil plans. Initially, the terrorists may burrow deeper into caves and other... hiding places. Our military action is also designed to clear the way for sustained, comprehensive and relentless operations to drive them out and bring them to justice.'

President Bush gives his reasons for invading Afghanistan, November 2001.

New allies, new enemies

When news of the terrorist attacks spread around the world, government leaders hurried to express their shock and horror, and to offer America their support. Even nations traditionally hostile to the USA, such as Libya and Iran, sent messages of sympathy. President Jacques Chirac of France (a frequent critic of American policy) declared, 'We are all Americans'.

Strong support

In return for these friendly words and promises of cooperation, America offered strong support to countries fighting terrorism on their own soil, including Russia, China and Israel. American government ministers stopped criticising harsh anti-terrorist actions, such as the use of a deadly knock-out gas to stun terrorists holding hostages in a theatre in Moscow, Russia. Before September 11th, they might have protested that these acts broke international agreements on human rights. On a visit to Russia, President Bush declared, 'When I was in high school, Russia was an enemy. Now high school students can know that Russia is a friend.'

President George W Bush thanks President Vladimir Putin of the Russian Federation for his support in the 'war on terror' (above). Putin's help signalled the beginning of an improved relationship between the USA and Russia.

Worldwide war

However, the attacks of September 11th meant that America had new enemies, as well as new friends. President Bush described his troops' invasion of Afghanistan as a new kind of conflict: a war on many fronts, against terrorists who operate in more than 60 different countries.

Suspicions

American diplomats warned all nations, including allies such as Saudi Arabia, not to tolerate Islamic extremists. They put pressure on the Palestinians to replace their leader, Yasser Arafat, because they believed he was not sufficiently 'tough against terrorists', and they alleged that Syria might be a 'state sponsoring terror'. They also kept a close watch on Pakistan, after Muslim terrorists there killed a respected American journalist and American embassy staff attending church. American army commanders made precautionary plans to invade unstable states like Somalia, where they believed that al-Qaeda terrorists were hiding, planning further attacks.

Contrasting views

America's call for a worldwide war against terror provoked contrasting reactions in many other lands. In Britain, the strongly pro-American government passed new laws giving police the right to imprison terrorist suspects before they had committed any crimes. Governments in Indonesia and the Philippines also cracked down on terrorist groups related to al-Queda. But many nations protested when American troops imprisoned hundreds of suspected terrorists from Afghanistan at Guantanamo Bay in Cuba. And Fidel Castro, the communist Cuban leader and America's

SUPPORT *from friends*

'*The entire international community should unite in the struggle against terrorism.*'
President Vladimir Putin of Russia

'*We, the democracies of the world, are going to have to come together to fight and eradicate this evil completely from our world.*'

British Prime Minister Tony Blair

'*An attack on one is an attack on all...*'

Lord Robertson, Secretary General of NATO (the North Atlantic Treaty Organization - a military alliance of European countries, Canada and the USA)

The Cuban leader Fidel Castro (above) was highly critical of the reaction by America's leaders to the attacks in the USA.

SYMPATHY *from enemies*

'Irrespective of the conflict with America, it is a human duty to show sympathy with the American people, and be one with them at these horrifying and awesome events which are bound to awaken human conscience.'

Libyan leader Moammar Gadhafi

[We offer] 'deep regret and sympathy... It is an international duty to try and undermine terrorism.'

President Mohammad Khatami of Iran

long-time enemy, said that America's reaction to the events of September 11th was 'worse than the original attacks'. Many observers felt dismay as American foreign policy became increasingly tough and hardline. They wondered whether America was squandering the sympathy it had received on September 11th, 2001.

'Axis of evil' In January 2002, after defeating the Taliban in Afghanistan, President Bush gave a speech

listing other countries that he believed supported terrorism. They included North Korea, Iran and Iraq. He called them 'an axis of evil', and promised that any terrorists they sheltered would be hunted down.

A monument in North Korea depicts the communist struggle (below). The country is on the USA's 'axis of evil' list of hostile states.

'What America is tasting now is something insignificant compared to what we have tasted for scores of years. Our nation (the Islamic world) has been tasting this humiliation and this degradation for more than 80 years. Its sons are killed, its blood is shed, its sanctuaries are attacked and no-one hears and no-one heeds.'

Looking back at the events of September 11, Osama bin Laden explains why he thinks the terrorist attacks were justified.

'We will pursue nations that provide aid or safe haven to terrorism. Every nation in every region now has a decision to make. Either you are with us, or you are with the terrorists.'

President Bush calls on other nations to join the war on terror.

George Bush chats to British Prime Minister Tony Blair prior to the second Gulf War.

Prior to America's invasion of Iraq in 2003, United Nations weapons inspectors had been scouring the country looking for weapons of mass destruction.

out Iraq, a former ally of the USA, as a special danger. In 1990, Saddam Hussein, the Iraqi dictator, had invaded neighboring Kuwait in an attempt to get control of its vast oil reserves and sparked the first Gulf War. A broad U.S.-led international coalition defeated him within months, but did not oust him from power. Hussein remainded an enemy of the West, and after September 11th, the Americans started to accuse him of supporting Palestinian terrorists and building terrible weapons loaded with germs and poisonous gas.

America acts

Saddam Hussein was hated and feared by his own people, and had very few allies abroad. But many nations felt deeply uneasy about America's threat to attack Iraq without clear evidence that they had weapons of mass destruction, and without the agreement of the United Nations. Many supported America's 'worldwide war against terrorism', but did not think it was right for America, the strongest nation in the world, to attack other countries just because it suspected them of planning terrorist acts. But America, along with its close ally Britain and other smaller nations in support, went ahead with its plans. Their

WMD In the months that followed, American government officials issued further warnings. They declared that any nation that was found to have weapons of mass destruction (WMD) would be considered a threat to future world peace and a legitimate (lawful) target for attack. The Americans singled

troops invaded and took control of Iraq in Spring, 2003.

Reasons for war

Since September 11th, 2001, America and its allies have argued that their war on terrorism is justified. They hope that their massive military strength will one day defeat al-Qaeda, or at least stop any government or nation offering it support. Critics have seen these anti-terrorist actions in a different way. They claim that American-led wars, especially in Iraq, have been thinly disguised attempts to impose Western secular values on other countries, especially Muslim ones. They say that the wars have also been a bid to take control of the world's most valuable power resource, oil.

Tough tactics, human rights

America's critics also argue that, in the hunt for terrorist suspects since September 11th, 2001, the USA and its allies ignored some of their most cherished democratic values – especially the right of suspects to be believed innocent until proved guilty. America's determination to fight terrorism with tough tactics made many Americans feel proud of their nation's strength. But to others, it raised a worrying question. Because of worldwide terrorism, and the attempts to stop it, were human rights now just a luxury that no 21st-century state could afford?

A massive statue of Saddam Hussein is pictured against the smoke and flames of war in Iraq. After a campaign of precision-bombing Iraqi military targets, most of the country was in American and British hands within a month.

BIN LADEN *speaks*

'... senior officials have spoken in America, starting with the head of infidels worldwide, Bush. They have come out in force with their men, and have turned even the countries that belong to Islam with this treachery, and they want to wag their tail at God, to fight Islam, to suppress people in the name of terrorism...'

Osama bin Laden claims that America's war against terrorism is an excuse to take over Muslim lands.

On May 5th, 2003, President Bush claimed that 'al-Qaeda is on the run'. But before the end of that month, al-Qaeda terrorists had staged two new murderous attacks, killing and injuring hundreds of civilians in Saudi Arabia and Morocco. There were further terrorist scares in East Africa and Southeast Asia, plus suggestions that al-Qaeda was planning fresh operations within the USA.

A waiting game

Experts believe that most of these terrorist attacks were the work of al-Qaeda 'sleepers' – people who had been recruited long before September 11th, 2001. They had been ordered to stay hidden, leading quiet, unremarkable, lives until they were ordered to act. Experts also acknowledged that there were probably thousands of trained al-Qaeda supporters,

The disaster of September 11th is still fresh in most Americans' minds, and every year many honour the victims of the tragedy. These firefighters in Tennessee are remembering all those in the service who surrendered their lives while trying to save others.

Suspected terrorists were taken to Guantanamo Bay, Cuba (below). America declared them 'unlawful combatants', a unique status that denied them the same rights as ordinary prisoners-of-war.

WORLD *view*

Has the world changed since September 11th, 2001?

YES: 'My world has changed a great deal. I have become more proud of my country, even if the world seems to look at my country in a negative light.'
April Liesel, Los Angeles County, California, USA, September 11, 2002

NO: 'There has not been any change in the political philosophy, social set-up, business system, means of production, educational system, or views on human rights.. No-one is born a terrorist. It is resentment and helplessness that drives a man to resort to this action.'
Professor Mukhtar Ali Naqvi, Orlando, Florida, USA, September 11, 2002

ready and waiting to commit fresh terrorist outrages, in almost 40 countries. Although America and its allies had shown that they could easily win conventional wars, in Iraq and Afghanistan it seemed clear that they had not yet found a way of defeating the largest and best-organised terrorist organization the world had ever seen.

A 'fact of life'?

Faced with this threat, people began to ask, 'What should the world do next?' How should governments deal with terrorism? Did politicians, police, soldiers and citizens simply have to accept that terrorism was now 'a fact of life', like the weather? Or should they fight against it? If so, should they hunt down terrorists and terrorist suspects in any way they could, with 'no holds barred'? Or should nations that claimed to admire freedom and democracy continue to uphold justice, liberty and human rights?

Still in shock

In many ways, the international community has yet to recover from the shock of the World Trade Center terrorist attacks. Most ordinary men and women are still saddened and horrified by terrorism. Few support terrorist attacks — even if they sympathize with

the terrorists' aims. But events since September 11th, 2001, have suggested that massive military firepower alone cannot stop terrorism. Some people are already looking for another way to bring peace, through political negotiations and economic reforms.

Time will tell

People looking for alternative solutions to the threat of terrorism understand that removing the injustices that make people decide to become terrorists will not solve the worldwide terror problem overnight, or abolish al-Qaeda. Sadly, there will always be activists with extreme religious or political views who will not agree to any sort of peaceful compromise. But to some, ending injustice, bringing hope, and working for equality seem to offer the chance of a better future for us all. Only time will tell if they are right.

Do peace talks stand a chance? In June 2003, a poster in Jerusalem urges Jews to reject President Bush's 'roadmap' — a plan that aims to reach a peace settlement between Israel and the Palestinians, and establish an independent Palestinian state (above).

THE WAY *forward*

'It is a sad confirmation that despite the rhetoric [fine words] and technological advances of modern human beings, violence is still the preferred method of dealing with problems. More violence will not solve the problem and power should not be measured in terms of military strength. The only way that September 11 could possibly change the world is if it caused us to wake up to the fact that we all share this planet and that peace is NOT achieved through war.'
Beth Strachan, Vancouver, Canada, September 11th, 2002

1200 BC–1896

- *c 1200 BC:* Jewish prophet Moses leads the Hebrew people into Canaan (land east of the Mediterranean Sea). They believe it is the 'Promised Land,' given to them by God.

- *c AD 570–632:* Lifetime of the Prophet Muhammad, an Arabian religious teacher. Muslims believe he was God's greatest messenger, and the last.

- *1098–1197:* Christian soldiers (Crusaders) occupy Holy Land.

- *1789–1793:* Word 'terrorist' first used in describing the mass murder of civilians during the French Revolution.

- *1880–1953:* Lifetime of Abd al-Aziz Ibn Saud, who campaigned for independence for Arabia and supported the strict Wahhabi movement for Islamic religious reform.

1897–1946

- *1897:* First Zionist Congress calls for a separate independent Jewish homeland.

- *1917:* British Foreign Secretary issues statement (the 'Balfour Declaration') supporting an independent Jewish state.

- *1932:* Saudi Arabia becomes an independent state. It grows rich after oil is discovered there in 1938.

- *1941:* American President Franklin D Roosevelt makes speech proclaiming human rights to the 'Four Freedoms' (freedom of speech, freedom of expression, freedom of worship, freedom from want and fear).

1947–1978

- *1947:* United Nations divides Palestine into Jewish and Arab states.

- *1948:* Israel becomes independent.

- *1967:* Israel occupies the West Bank, where many Palestinians live.

- *1970s:* Palestinian terrorists hijack aircraft in Jordan, and kill members of the Israeli Olympic Team in Munich, Germany.

- *1976:* The Hamas Islamic Resistance Movement is founded by Sheikh Yassin Ahmad. Originally non-militant, it began using increasingly violent means during the 1990s, including the tactic of suicide bombing.

1979–1986

- *1979:* Soviet troops invade Afghanistan. Afghan mujahedin (Muslim guerrilla fighters) declare a holy war against them.

- *1979:* Muslim fundamentalists overthrow the Shah (king) in Iran. Radical Islamic leader Ayatollah Khomeini returns from exile to lead the Islamic Revolution.

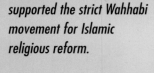

1987–1993

• 1987: An intifada (uprising) is launched by Palestinians in protest against Israeli occupation of the West Bank and the Gaza Strip. They kill many Israeli civilians in suicide-bomb attacks. Israelis retaliate by demolishing buildings where Palestinian terrorists are suspected of hiding.

• 1989: Saudi Arabian millionaire Osama bin Laden founds al-Qaeda ('the Base') to unite all Muslims and set up a world Islamic government.

• 1993: Muslim terrorists, suspected of links with al-Qaeda, attack American army helicopters in Somalia.

• 1993: al-Qaeda is suspected of planting a small bomb that explodes beneath the World Trade Center in New York, USA.

1994–2000

• 1994: Afghan Muslim religious teacher Mullah Mohammad Omar founds the Taliban ('God's Students') religious movement in Afghanistan.

• 1995: A plot is uncovered in which the al-Qaeda group intended to kill the then US President Bill Clinton in the Philippines.

• 1996: The Taliban take control of Afghanistan, and introduce strict Muslim laws throughout the country.

• 1996: Osama bin Laden is expelled from Saudi Arabia, and moves to the Taliban-controlled country of Afghanistan.

• 1998: al-Qaeda declares that it is the duty of all Muslims to kill American citizens and their allies.

• 1998: al-Qaeda blows up the American embassies in Kenya and Tanzania, killing many people.

• 2000: Muslim terrorists linked to al-Qaeda attack the American Navy ship USS Cole, while it is in harbour in the Middle Eastern country of Yemen.

2001–2002

• September 11th, 2001: Muslim terrorists hijack four civilian flights in America. Two fly into the twin towers of the World Trade Center, New York, and cause them to collapse; one crashes into the Pentagon in Washington DC, and the other crashes in a field. Links with al-Qaeda suspected.

• September–October 2001: President Bush promises to bring terrorists to justice. Americans receive support from many world leaders, including its former enemy, Russia. New Department of Homeland Security set up in America. New security checks on air passengers. Mysterious anthrax attacks spread panic across America.

• October 2001: American-led attack Afghanistan. The Taliban disperse.

• January 2002: President Bush makes speech naming North Korea, Iran and Iraq as an 'axis of evil'.

2002–

• October 2002: Muslim terrorists fighting for independence from Russia in Chechnya hold hostages in a theatre in Moscow, Russia.

• October 2002: Muslim terrorists linked to al-Qaeda attack nightclubs in Bali, Indonesia, causing many deaths.

• March 2003: America and its allies, including Britain, Australia and Poland, invade Iraq.

• May 2003: President Bush claims that 'al-Qaeda is on the run'. Days later, al-Qaeda terrorists attack civilians in Saudi Arabia and Morocco.

al-Qaeda 'The Base'. Terrorist organisation founded by Osama bin Laden in 1989 with the aim of uniting all Muslims and establishing a world Islamic government. Al-Qaeda's two main grievances are the presence of 'infidels' in Arabia, the birthplace of the prophet Muhammad, and the failure of the West to offer the Palestinians an independent state.

anthrax A fatal bacterial disease, originally transmitted to humans from sheep and cattle. Anthrax may be manufactured as a biological weapon and can kill if inhaled.

axis of evil Term given by President George W Bush to the countries deemed actively hostile to American interests, namely Iran, Iraq and North Korea.

biological weapons Toxins, bacteria or viruses manufactured for use in warfare. Biological weapons probably form a substantial part of many states' arsenals.

Chechnya Region in the south-west of the Russian Federation where ethnic Chechens are fighting for independence from Moscow. Chechen terrorist groups have made a number of attacks against Russian targets, most prominently in October 2002 when a Moscow theatre was seized and its audience taken hostage.

CIA The Central Intelligence Agency. America's intelligence-gathering organisation operating around the world.

crusade Originally, a medieval military expedition to recover the Holy Land from the Muslims. Today, a term used to mean a strong campaign in favour of a moral cause.

dictatorship A state in which all power rests in the hands of one individual, the dictator.

ETA A terrorist movement campaigning for independence for the Basque region of northern Spain and south-west France.

F15s The fighter jet aircraft scrambled on September 11th, 2001 – to patrol the skies over the Northeastern USA after the attack on the World Trade Center in New York.

FBI The Federal Bureau of Investigation. America's nationwide law-enforcement organisation.

fundamentalism The strict observance of the ancient or traditional beliefs of a religion.

guerrilla A member of an independent rebel group fighting for a particular cause.

Hamas A Palestinian resistance movement founded by Sheikh Yassin Ahmad in 1976. It is notable for its use of violent tactics, particularly that of suicide bombing.

hijack To seize control – for example, of an aircraft – and force it to a different destination.

Holy Land A region of the Middle East divided between Syria, Israel, Jordan and the disputed Palestinian territories. The Holy Land is sacred to people from three of the world's great faiths – Judaism, Christianity and Islam.

Homeland Security Department set up by President George W Bush in the wake of the events of September 11th, 2001, in order to improve America's internal security.

infidel Name used by Muslim fundamentalists to describe all non-Muslims.

IRA The Irish Republican Army. Terrorist organisation originally founded in 1919. Its aim is to unite Northern Ireland (part of the United Kingdom) with the Republic of Ireland in the south. The IRA's tactics have included bombing campaigns, kidnappings and guerilla warfare.

jihad An Arabic term meaning 'holy war'. Muslim scholars point out that it also refers to many other kinds of struggle, such as trying to work well, or lead an honest life.

Middle East A large region of Southwest Asia and North Africa, stretching from the Mediterranean to Pakistan and including the Arabian Peninsula. It comprises mainly Arabic-speaking peoples.

Molotov cocktail A crude, thrown explosive device made of flammable liquid in a bottle.

Maoists Followers of the teachings of Chinese communist leader Mao Zedong (1893–1976). Terrorists in Nepal hold Maoist political beliefs, as do the 'Shining Path' guerrillas in Peru.

mujahedin Muslim guerrilla fighters. These were prominent as an effective guerrilla fighting force in Afghanistan after the Soviet Union invaded the country in 1979.

NATO The North Atlantic Treaty Organisation. A treaty made in April 1949 in which Western European states entered into a military alliance with America to provide each other with mutual military assistance in the event of an attack — especially from the apparent threat posed by communist countries in eastern Europe.

NORAD North American Aerospace Defense Command. The military organization that guards the skies over Canada and America.

pre-emptive action Controversial American practice of taking military action against states suspected of promoting terrorism or possessing weapons of mass destruction, even though there may be no evidence of such states' intentions or capabilities.

Promised Land In the Jewish faith, the land promised to the Jews by God. The land of Canaan, between the river Jordan and the Mediterranean Sea.

roadmap The name given to the American-sponsored Israeli-Palestinian peace initiative of 2003, by which a series of dates and steps toward peace is to be agreed by both sides with the eventual aim of peace and an independent Palestinian state.

secular Non-religious.

shariyah Muslim holy law, based on the teachings of the Muslim holy book, the Qur'an.

Shining Path A movement of Maoist guerillas in Peru. During the 1990s they were responsible for terrorising and killing thousands of people, mainly in rural areas.

Soviet Union A country formed from the territories of the Russian Empire after the Russian Revolution of October 1917. Also called the USSR (the Union of Soviet Socialist Republics). The Soviet Union broke up in 1991.

suicide bomber A terrorist who deliberately kills himself or herself in the act of detonating a bomb. Some Muslim fundamentalists hope to become martyrs through such an act.

Taliban 'God's students'. Fundamentalist Muslim movement founded by Afghan religious teacher, Mullah Mohammad Omar in 1994. The Taliban at first fought lawlessness and corruption, and introduced a very strict Islamic regime in Afghanistan, banning music and any form of occupation for women outside the home.

Tamil Tigers Sri Lankan terrorist guerillas. Their aim is to establish an independent homeland for the ethnic Tamil minority in northern Sri Lanka, free from control by the majority Sinhalese. Throughout the 1970s and 1980s, they set up camps to train terrorists, and carried out many suicide bombing attacks.

terrorism The use of violence or intimidation for political ends. Widespread public fear of random atrocities is terrorism's main aim and effect.

United Nations An international peace-seeking organisation, based in New York.

Wahhabism A strict Islamic religious reform movement, which aims to purify Islam.

UN weapons inspectors Officials sent by the United Nations to search and account for certain types of weapons in countries not permitted by the UN to keep such weapons.

WMD Weapons of Mass Destruction. These may include biological, chemical or nuclear weapons.

A

Abd al-Aziz Ibn Saud 14, 42

Abraham 12

Afghanistan 20, 21, 34, 35, 36, 37, 41, 42, 43, 45

Alexander II, Tsar 16

al-Qaeda 19, 20, 21, 33, 35, 37, 39, 40, 41, 43, 44

    sleepers 40

American Airlines 22, 23, 26

ambulance crews 4, 25, 28, 29, 31

Annan, Kofi 6, 31

anthrax 33, 44

Arafat, Yasser 31, 36

Australia 8, 43

axis of evil 37, 43, 44

Ayatollah Khomeini 42

B

B-2 Stealth Bombers 5

Balfour, Arthur 14

    Balfour Declaration 42

Bali 43

Basques 18

Belfast 18

bin Laden, Osama 6, 7, 15, 17, 20, 32, 33, 34, 35, 37, 39, 43, 44

Blair, Tony 36, 38

Boston 22, 23

Britain 14, 17, 37, 38, 43

Bush, George W 9, 24, 27, 29, 30, 31, 32, 33, 35, 36, 37, 38, 39, 40, 41, 43, 44

C

Canada 45

capitalism 8

Capitol 26

car bombs 18

Chechnya 18, 43, 44

China 11, 36

Chirac, Jacques 36

Christianity 12

Christians 12, 13, 15, 16, 33

CIA (Central Intelligence Agency)
    32, 44

Clinton, Bill 21, 43

Coca-Cola 8

cocaine 19

Cold War, the 8, 20

Colombia 19

communists 11, 16

Crusades 14, 15

Cuba 37, 40

D

democracy 8, 11

Dome of the Rock 12

E

Egypt 12, 14

ETA 18, 44

Europe 11, 14, 36

F

FBI (Federal Bureau of Investigation) 24, 32, 44

fighter jets 22, 28, 35, 44

firefghters 4, 5, 25, 28, 29, 30, 31

First Zionist Congress 14, 42

founding fathers 11

France 14, 18, 36

French Revolution 16, 42

    The Terror 16

G

Gadhafi, Moammar 37

Gaza Strip 20, 43

geologists 13

Germany 9, 42

Giuliani, Rudolph 29, 31

Ground Zero 30, 31

Guantanamo Bay 37, 40

guillotines 16

H

Hamas 17, 42, 44

hijacks 4, 16, 17, 22, 23, 24, 27, 42, 44

Holy Land 12, 13, 14, 42, 44

hostages 16

House of Representatives 11

Hudson River 30

Hussein, Saddam 6, 38, 39

I

immigrants 11

India 14

Indonesia 37, 43

Internet 5

intifada 20, 43

Iran 6, 11, 12, 13, 14, 36, 38, 42, 43, 44

    Shah of Iran 42

Iraq 6, 12, 13, 14, 17, 38, 40, 43, 44

ISAF (International Security Assistance Force) 34

Isaac 12

Islam 12, 14, 15, 34, 35

Islamic Revolution 14, 20, 42

isolationism 9

Israel 6, 12, 14, 15, 20, 36, 41, 42, 44

J

Javidnama 11

Jerusalem 12, 41

Jesus Christ 12

Jews 12, 13, 14, 15, 21, 33

jihad 21, 44

Jordan 12, 21, 42, 44

Judaism 12

K

Kabul 34, 35

Kenya 16, 17, 21, 43

Kikuyu 16, 17

Kuwait 13

L

League of Nations 14

Le Sueur, Marian 9

Libya 36, 37

Logan Airport 22

Los Angeles 22, 24, 26, 40

Loyalists 18, 19

M

Mao Zedong 19, 45

Mau Mau 16

Mecca 12

Medina 12

Middle East 6, 12, 13, 14, 15,

17, 19, 44
Mohammad Atta 22
Mohammad Khatami 37
Molotov cocktail 18, 45
Morocco 40, 43
Moscow 36, 43, 44
Moses 12, 42
mosques 12
Muhammad 12, 32, 42, 44
Muhammad Ibn Abd al-Wahhab 15
Muhammad Iqbal 11
mujahedin 14, 21, 45
Mullah Mohammad Omar 34, 43, 45
multinational corporations 10
Munich 42
Muslims 6, 11, 12, 13, 14, 15, 18, 20, 24, 32, 35, 39, 42, 43, 44, 45

N

Narodnaya Volya (The People's Will) 16
Nationalists 19
NATO (North Atlantic Treaty Organization) 36, 45
Nepal 19, 45
New York 4, 7, 11, 21, 22, 23, 27, 28, 30, 43, 44, 45
New York Stock Exchange 10
NORAD (North American Aerospace Defense Command) 22, 45
Northern Ireland 18, 19
North Korea 37, 43, 44

O

oil 13, 14, 42
Orlando 40
Ottoman Empire 13, 14

P

Pakistan 15, 34, 36, 44
Palestine 12, 14, 15, 17, 32, 42
Pentagon 4, 26, 30, 43
Persian Gulf 13
Peru 19, 45
Philippines 37, 43
Philistines 13
pilgrims 12
Pittsburgh 27
Poland 43
police 4, 25, 28, 29, 30, 41
Pope John Paul II 21, 31
Powell, Colin 34
prisoners-of-war 40
prophets 12
Protestants 18
Putin, Vladimir 36

Q

Qur'an 14, 44

R

religion 10, 14
roadmap to peace 41, 43, 45
Robertson, Lord 36
Romans 13
Roosevelt, Franklin D 10, 42
Russia 8, 14, 18, 20, 36, 43

S

Samaritans 13
Saudi Arabia 11, 13, 14, 15, 20, 36, 40, 42, 43
Senate 11
Sharon, Ariel 31
shariyah 14, 44
Shining Path 45
Sinhalese 17, 45
smallpox 33
Solomon 12
Somalia 21, 37, 43
Southeast Asia 40
Spain 18
Sri Lanka 17, 45
Statue of Liberty 11
stocks and shares 10
suicide bombers 16, 42, 43, 45
Syria 12, 36, 44

T

Taliban 20, 21, 34, 35, 38, 43, 45
Tamils 17
  'Tigers' 17, 45
tanks 34
Tanzania 21, 43
tawhid 15
taxes 8
temples 12
Thurber, James 33
Turkey 13, 14

U

United Airlines 22, 24, 27
United Nations 7, 14, 15, 38, 42, 45

unlawful combatants 40
US Constitution 11
US Customs 32
US Federal Aviation Administration 22
USS Cole 21, 43

V

Vancouver 41

W

Wahhabi 14, 42, 45
warlords 34, 35
Washington DC 4, 26, 27, 30, 43, 44
weapons inspectors 38, 45
welfare benefits 8
West Bank 17, 18, 20, 42, 43
White House 26, 27
WMD (Weapons of Mass Destruction) 38, 45
World Trade Center 4, 21, 22, 23, 24, 25, 26, 28, 29, 30, 31, 41, 43, 44
  north tower 22, 23, 24, 28
  south tower 24, 25, 28
(WTO) World Trade OrganiZation 10
World War I 13
World War II 8

Y

Yassin Ahmad, Sheikh 17, 42, 44
Yemen 43

Z

Zimbabwe 8

Copyright © ticktock Entertainment Ltd 2003
First published in Great Britain in 2003 by ticktock Media Ltd.,
Unit 2, Orchard Business Centre, North Farm Road, Tunbridge Wells, Kent, TN2 3XF

ISBN 1 86007 419 7 pbk
ISBN 1 86007 426 X hbk
Printed in Taiwan

A CIP catalogue record for this book is available from the British Library.

We would like to thank: Tall Tree Ltd, Lizzy Bacon and Ed Simkins for their assistance.

10 9 8 7 6 5 4 3 2 1

Picture Credits